SCOTLAND

FROM THE AIR

SCOTLAND
FROM THE AIR

JASON HAWKES

EBURY
PRESS

First published in Great Britain in 2001

1 3 5 7 9 10 8 6 4 2

Ebury Press

Random House, 20 Vauxhall Bridge Road, London SW1V 2SA

Random House Australia (Pty) Limited
20 Alfred Street, Milsons Point, Sydney, New South Wales 2061, Australia

Random House New Zealand Limited
18 Poland Road, Glenfield, Auckland 10, New Zealand

Random House (Pty) Limited
Endulini, 5a Jubilee Road, Parktown 2193, South Africa

The Random House Group Limited Reg. No. 954009

www.randomhouse,co.uk

Papers used by Ebury Press are natural, recyclable products made from wood grown in sustainable forests.

A CIP catalogue record for this book is available from the British Library

ISBN 0 09 187904 3

Designed by David Fordham

Typeset in Trajan and Fournier by MATS, Southend-on-Sea, Essex
Printed and bound in Portugal by Printer Portuguesa

CONTENTS

INTRODUCTION
SCOTLAND

'*IN ORDER TO teach people to see things in a new light, it is essential to photograph normal objects with which they are familiar from entirely unexpected angles and positions ... The most instructive viewpoints from which to depict modern life were those from above, from below and on the diagonal.*'

ALEXANDRO RODECHENKO, 1927

If aerial photography is the means of showing people how to look at things in a different light, there can't be a better subject than Scotland. When dealing with any subject, it is often best to get the generalizations out of the way first and so, let's admit it, haggis, heather, men in kilts, tartan and bagpipes have all been standard fare for many years when thinking about Scotland. People drink whisky and eat shortbread. Glitzy Hollywood films have perpetuated the myth of a barbaric race, thinly disguised as fiercely nationalistic, and grimly 'realistic' films from this

side of the water have portrayed contemporary Scottish youth in a more apathetic drug-induced state. As with any stereotype, there are probably grains of truth in all of the above but none explain the full story. It is only when you look at the bigger picture – taking into consideration social, industrial and cultural history – that a coherent sense of the country appears. Aerial photography is capable of doing the pictorial equivalent of this, quite literally looking at the bigger picture. From the air, objects that are seen every day are metamorphosed into something new and often quite unrecognizable, but how they fit together becomes increasingly clear and exciting to contemplate.

The first ventures into aerial photography drew plenty of reproach, perhaps unsurprisingly, as photography itself had been subject to some cuttingly harsh criticism. For example, after Daguerre made details of his photography process public on 19 August 1839, a newspaper report in the *Leipzig City Advertiser* stated: 'The wish to capture evanescent reflections

DUNCANSBY HEAD AND EDINBURGH

Left Surrounded by dramatic cliffs, the lighthouse at Duncansby Head has been a necessity over the years as the water that divides the mainland from the Orkneys is one of the most treacherous in the world. Its strong tides, combined with a high wind speed and a rocky sea bed, can cause deep whirlpools and terrifying towers of water.

Above Edinburgh has always dominated the Lothian counties and the rock on which the castle sits, an extinct volcano, has long been strategically important.

is not only impossible ... but the mere desire alone, the will to do so, is blasphemy. God created man in His own image, and no man-made machine may fix the image of God. Is it possible that God should have abandoned His eternal principles, and allowed a Frenchman ... to give to the world an invention of the Devil?'

By the time experiments into aerial photography were beginning in the 1860s, criticism centred around the fact that the camera actually appeared to lie by distorting the view, and that people could not possibly find beautiful what they could not relate to. Supporters returned with the view that the pictures may not conform to the known rules of perspective, but this was no barrier to considering them attractive. Today, technological advancements in areas such as aeronautics and art have meant that not only are we able to relate to a wide variety of perspectives, but this often serves to enhance our understanding and pleasure of a subject.

Scotland is an area that lends itself well to the medium of aerial photography, purely because the landscape is so varied. Its rugged coastline is so indented and craggy that its aggregate length is estimated at 2300 miles, even though the mainland's maximum width is 154 miles and length 275 miles. With a mainland well known for its lochs and mountains, Scotland also has 790 islands of which around 130 are inhabited. It is home to a plethora of diverse wildlife, including a rich birdlife, and yet is also the location for some of the remotest and most barren landscape in the United Kingdom. And then there are the many towns, cities, villages and man-made monuments spread across the country. Put another way, there was never going to be a problem with lack of subject matter for this book.

Present-day Scotland (as well as the aforementioned stereotypes) is largely a result of what has gone before and so it is worth dipping into its history. There is very little known about the first settlers in Scotland, although they were probably cave-dwelling hunter-gatherers who collected shellfish from the shorelines to eat. Similarly, little is known about the next wave of settlers, the so-called Beaker People who placed pottery beakers filled with drink in the tombs of their dead to aid them on

their way to their next life. It was the Romans who produced the first written accounts of the people of Scotland and the second-century Greco-Egyptian geographer Ptolemy who drew up the first known map. So, recorded history really started around 80 AD when a Roman army led by Agricola ventured north to the Firth of Tay to size up the possibility of defeating the troublesome Caledonii of the north – a fierce, heavily-tattooed warrior race known as the Picts.

By the fifth century, there were four main tribes who occupied various parts of Scotland – the Picts, the Scots, the Angles and the Britons. Warfare between the four of them was intermittent over the centuries although the introduction of Christianity, attractive to the pagan Kings as it seemed to offer them supernatural powers, and exploitation of marriages between the two main tribes (the Picts and the Scots), meant the Scots eventually emerged triumphant. By 1034, almost all of what we call Scotland was under the rule of King Malcolm II.

From the twelfth century, and probably earlier, Scotland had a closer affiliation with Europe than with England. Trade with the Netherlands flourished and it is even thought that the game of golf, so dearly loved in Scotland today, originally came from Holland. Scottish fashion and architecture were borrowed from France and cultural contacts were nurtured. England was simply a threat to Scottish autonomy.

When Alexander III tragically died in an accident in 1286, the situation spiralled downhill. The peace that Scotland had enjoyed ended when Edward I attempted to subjugate Scotland, resulting in an astronomical amount of bloodshed when he massacred the entire population of Berwick. The resulting troubles led to the emergence of the now legendary William Wallace as a national hero. Wallace's initial battle against the English took place at Stirling (meaning the place of strife) in 1297 and from here he stormed up the Scottish east coast capturing Forfar, Dundee, Brechin, Montrose Castle and Dunnottar Castle. Eventually betrayed and executed in London in 1305, William Wallace is still remembered for his brave tirade against the English and a statue dedicated to him outside His Majesty's Theatre in Aberdeen bears an inscription allegedly told to Wallace by his Uncle: 'I will tell you a truth, liberty is the best of all things, my son, never live under any slavish bond.'

Political problems lasted until well into the eighteenth century and even the Jacobite rebellion (when first the 'Old Pretender' and then his son 'Bonnie Prince Charlie' tried to regain the British throne for the House of Stuart) culminated in the messy Battle of Culloden. However, regardless of the physical battles that have plagued Scotland throughout its history, the single event that has most shaped the landscape as it stands today must surely be the Clearances. Extensive sheep farming was incompatible with a high peasant population so between 1760 and 1886 landlords simply evicted tenants off their land, often forcibly. The Countess of Sutherland forced 15,000 people off her million-acre estate, and if they refused, their houses were burnt down in front of them. The crofters suffered poverty and famine and many emigrated to America and Canada. The re-population of the Highlands never took place, and today vast areas of deserted wilderness is one of its defining features.

Intellectually, Scotland came into its own in the eighteenth century and prolific writers, philosophers, architects, scientists and inventors found endless inspiration during a period that has become known as the Scottish Enlightenment. Among them were David Hume, whose work aroused Kant from his 'dogmatic slumber', the endlessly quoted poet Robert Burns, and the great novelist Sir Walter Scott. These may be the best known but the list is almost endless, and the Scots achieved huge advances in almost every sector including the invention of the steam hammer (John McAdam) and the invention of the waterproof 'mac' (Charles MacIntosh).

Regardless of the Clearances, industrialization meant that Scotland appeared to be prospering. Ironworks were built, new shipyards were opened and new coal mines were sunk. The pace didn't slacken until the First World War when the industry sector almost collapsed. Whereas 750,000 tons of shipping was built on the Clyde in 1900, by 1933 this had fallen to 56,000 tons and mass unemployment followed. It wasn't until oil was discovered in 1970 that the economy picked up again.

Today, Scotland is acknowledged as a place where art and architecture are taken seriously. As the country's capital, Edinburgh is a prime example of this with its drama and comedy festival attracting hundreds of visitors each year. Comparable to the world's most beautiful cities, it was mainly built in a single creative burst between 1767 and 1840 and the neo-classical new town was essentially conceived by the forceful Lord Mayor who ran a competition for the design. An unknown 22-year-old called James Craig won this competition, and his plan, designed around the symbolism of the union of Scotland and England, was carried out. Glasgow also deserves an honorable mention at this point as it has recently been voted both City of Culture and UK City of Architecture and Design, was home to the Glasgow Boys who shook up the art establishment and was also the base of architectural genius Charles Rennie Mackintosh.

If you are more interested in the great outdoors, you won't be disappointed. After all, regardless of the variety of wildlife, lochs, hills and mountains to be found, no introduction to Scotland would be complete without the mention of its most famous and best-loved inhabitant, the Loch Ness Monster. If she does exist, she is hundreds of years old – the first recorded sighting was by St Columba but there have since been numerous reported sightings of the enigmatic Nessie. There have also been reports of another monster living in the depths of Loch Morar, the less well-known Morag, which, depending on how you look at it, may or may not increase the likelihood of such a creature existing. Certainly, there is enough food in the ecosystem of both lochs to support large whale-like creatures, perhaps such as a zeuglodon – a primitive snake-like whale, which has long since been assumed extinct. However, many of the images of Nessie that have been captured on film are easy to explain away as playing otters or a mass of dead plant matter.

Unfortunately, there are no images of Nessie on the following pages, but there are plenty of photographs that will capture your imagination just the same. And no one will blame you for having a second glance at the picture of Loch Ness on page 98, just in case.

CASTLES, HOUSES AND MONUMENTS

POPULAR FILMS SUCH as *Braveheart* play on the image of the Scottish as being a fiercely nationalistic race with a penchant for a bloody battle. For all its historical inaccuracies and Hollywood glitz, the film does have a point. The Scottish determination to fight for what is theirs has a long and traceable history, starting with the Picts, or 'painted ones'. In around 80 AD, when organized troops of highly trained Roman soldiers turned up to conquer Scotland, they lost their entire ninth legion in a bloody massacre waged by hostile tribes who knew the terrain well enough to disappear into the surroundings and lay fatal ambushes.

The Picts were the most powerful race in Scotland for almost 1000 years, although they were constantly challenged by three other races: the Angles, the Britons and the Scots. It wasn't until 1034 that they were successfully united although internal fighting weakened them to external attacks, not only from overseas visitors but also from the seemingly ever-present English armies. In the midst of such a tempestuous climate, it is unsurprising that those who lived in Scotland felt such a need to fortify.

Between the eleventh and the seventeenth centuries (before the introduction of gunpowder weakened their ability to protect), castles were essential for kings, lords and barons, not only for protection but also to demonstrate their importance in the area. Over the years, castles continued to be improved and updated. Any vulnerable areas were identified and changed, so that, for example, corners and doors – which were seen as weak points so castles – were built with round walls and drawbridges.

What is left today is a veritable playground for the architecture of defence; keeps, castles, forts, garrisons and watchtowers are strewn across the countryside, alongside other structures of religious or social importance. The locations are as dramatic as they are varied – obviously strategic positioning was paramount when they were conceived, and the impact of the sites have not lessened with age. Between them, the selection of structures photographed over the following pages have been built, re-built, captured, destroyed, abandoned, neglected and restored.

CASTLE CAMPBELL AND DRYBURGH ABBEY

Left The picturesque Castle Campbell stands in an impressive setting above the wooded hills of Dollar. It was once named Castle Gloom, unfortunately a derivation of an old Gaelic word rather than an evocative moniker.

Above Not to be outdone in setting, Dryburgh Abbey is bordered by the River Tweed and is famous for being the burial place of Sir Walter Scott. The abbey was burnt down by Edward II and restored by Robert I.

EILEAN DONAN CASTLE, LOCH DUICH AND STALKER CASTLE, LOCH LINNHE

Above Situated on a small rocky peninsula at the confluence of three lochs, Eilean Donan Castle was originally built on the site of an ancient fort around 1230 but, after being destroyed by English warships in the early 1700s, it was for a long time nothing more than a ruin. Restoration started at the beginning of the twentieth century.

Right The castle as it appears today was built by the Stewarts of Appin a few hundred years later. It changed hands only when it was lost in a drunken bet by the 7th chief of Appin, and ownership passed to the Campbells until it was abandoned in 1780.

KEISS CASTLE

One of the earliest inhabited places in Scotland is thought to be pinpointed by the sweeping coastline of Sinclair's Bay. At the northern point of this bay sits the remnants of Keiss Castle, precariously positioned at the edge of a cliff. Built by the Sinclairs in the sixteenth century, it served as a home for the Caithness Earls, and William Sinclair, the founder of the first Baptist church in Scotland, lived here. It was abandoned in 1775 for the new Keiss Castle and today the thin walls are crumbling into the sea.

DUNNOTTAR CASTLE

Named after the Pict for 'fort of the low country' (*Dun Fother*), Dunnottar Castle is dramatically located at Stonehaven on a solitary rock jutting into the sea. The coastal area around the castle is known as The Mearns and the castle provided a simple way to patrol what was once the easiest way to Moray and beyond. Its rocky promontory is extremely unusual, dating back around 400 million years to the erosion of the Grampians. The castle, however, is slightly younger – most of what remains is from 900 AD. It has been witness to some bloody events: in 1685, 167 covenanters were imprisoned, tortured and left to rot in the dungeons here and this was where William Wallace burnt the English Plantagenet garrison in 1297.

STIRLING CASTLE

Left A St Albans monk once drew a map of Britain, which represented Scotland as two separate lands joined only by Stirling Bridge. Though this representation was unfaithful, Stirling was once surrounded by marshland, making it the only accessible route between the north and south of Scotland. For this reason it became strategically prudent for a stronghold to be built, although Stirling's first fortress was built in pre-historic times. This impregnable structure dominates the town, and would have provided a daunting deterrent for any would-be attackers, not least due to the 77-m (250-ft) drop down the side of the crag. Nevertheless, this area has acted as a backdrop to many battles between the Scottish, desperate for their freedom, and the English, and the castle top provides views of seven battlefields.

EDINBURGH CASTLE

Right As the second most visited monument in Britain (the first being the Tower of London) you would expect there to be something special about Edinburgh Castle – and it doesn't disappoint. Not only does it shape the skyline of Edinburgh but the dramatic topography from the castle across the city is a worthy second best to seeing it from a helicopter. It is impossible to escape from the castle's colourful history, stretching from the birthplace of King James VI of Scotland and James I of England to the resting place of the ancient Hònours of Scotland – a crown, sceptre and sword of state that symbolize Scotland's autonomy. However, best of all is the One O'clock Gun, which is fired at 1pm each day, except Sunday, and scares the living daylights out of you if you have lost track of time.

DRYBURGH ABBEY

Left Bordered by the River Tweed, Dryburgh Abbey is set in such a peacefully rural area that it is easy to imagine the serene monks of the Premonstratension Order going about their daily routines in contented silence. However, this land also bears the scars of a turbulent, violent past, which saw attacks from English Invaders from the thirteenth to the seventeenth centuries, as well as from the mosstroopers – the border bandits.

FLOORS CASTLE

Above As a privately owned home to the 10th Duke of Roxburgh, Floors Castle was the location of choice when Prince Andrew proposed to Sarah Ferguson in 1986. In the grounds stands a holly tree said to mark the spot where James II was killed when a cannon blew up during a siege in 1640.

POLTALLOCH HOUSE, SRATHCLYDE

Above The derelict mansion looks like the castle from the Sleeping Beauty fairytale, overgrown with creeping ivy and other greenery. Only time will tell if a Prince Charming will reinstate it to its former glory.

ACKERGILL TOWER

Right Ackergill Tower has certainly been rescued – the tower was thought to be beyond salvation when it was put up for sale in 1986 and bought by John and Arlette Banister. It was a stronghold of Clan Keith, and has in its time been plundered, seized, rescued, neglected and restored.

WALLACE MONUMENT

Left Set among the leaping ramparts of the Ochil Hills on the Abbey Craig, the distinctive Wallace Monument towers 68m (220ft) above the Forth Valley. It stands in tribute to William Wallace, the infamous normal-man-turned-hero who forged an army of peasants and townsmen to expel the English army from Scotland and led them to spectacular triumph in the 1298 Battle of Stirling. As a result of politics – he never found Royal backing – Wallace met an untimely death when he was betrayed and executed in London in 1305, but the monument, completed in 1856, commemorates his courage and conviction and displays his two-handed broadsword.

WATERLOO MONUMENT

Right Deep in the Borders, near Nisbet, Jedburgh, this tall, pencil thin and rather plain monument was erected in celebration of Wellington's victory of Waterloo. It is prominently sited above a great expanse of sparse countryside and was built on a whim by a marquis of Lothian with the help on his tenants. To the eyes of the more cynical among us, it commemorates the vast power and influence of the land-owning gentry as much as, if not more than, the victory at Waterloo.

PATTERNS OF NATURE

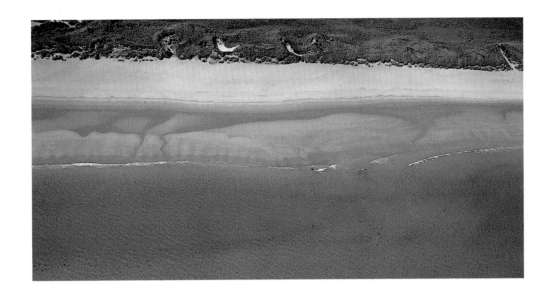

IF MAN IS NOTICEABLY absent in some of the more remote areas of Scotland, wildlife is anything but. When primitive man first appeared, all but the wettest and highest land would have been blanketed by forest. The post-glacial sun at the end of the Ice Age led to a more hospitable climate for nature, and the first mosses, scrubby willows and heather slowly developed into birch, junipers and oaks. Even though places like Sutherland and Caithness probably never supported more than basic scrubs, woodland was abundant in Scotland and with it came a rich variety of birds and animals.

Man has always had the urge to contain nature and use it to his best advantage, which has almost always meant destruction for wildlife. Even before the Clearances, landowners would burn woods to extend their space for sheep, oaks were reduced to charcoal when the smelting industry took off and pines were chopped down to be used as timber. Loss of the once plentiful forests led to soil erosion, and once their habitat had disappeared so too did many animals, including elk, lynx and bears.

If the only chance of breeding these lost animals again is to wait until cloning techniques are vastly improved, we can all console ourselves with the fact that there is still plenty to keep even the most avid nature-lover occupied. From free-ranging Highland deer to puffins to mountain saxifrages and gentians, Scotland is still home to exotic plants and rare wildlife. Conservation is serious business and Scotland contains more woodland now than at any time since the eighteenth century (even if most of it is fast-growing conifers).

In addition to the woodland there are also an increasing number of wildlife reserves and parks. Montrose Bay (see page 79), to pick a single example, provides a rich feeding ground for thousands of resident birds and migrant species. And, most importantly, there are conservation success stories to bring hope for the future of birds and wildlife in Britain. Although ospreys had been lost to Scotland since Edwardian times, after one pair came to nest in the Highlands in the 1950s the number today is closer to 30 pairs.

SINCLAIR'S BAY

The Caithness coast has many different features from cliffs and stacks to the long sandy beaches seen here. One of the best known parts of the coast is Sinclair's Bay. For many years it was one of the finest lobster and crab areas in Scotland. Although somewhat over-fished it still produces fine specimens and many small boats still put out creels. Surfers are drawn from all over Britain to enjoy the waves. The swells reach up to 6m (20ft) in winter although you have to love the sport then as the water temperature can go down to four degrees Celsius.

SEALS ON BEACH AT DORNOCH FIRTH AND SALMON FISHING ON MONTROSE BASIN

Left Seals (including the shy grey ones), whales, dolphins and porpoises are not an uncommon sight in Scotland, especially around the Grampian Coast, the Western Isles, the Moray Firth and the Cromarty Firth. While shy of people, the seals will often propel themselves up onto the sand if no one else is around.

Above Salmon has been caught, processed and exported from this area as far back as the Middle Ages. In the eighteenth century, Montrose started to trade with Billingsgate market in London. A few miles from Montrose there is an old-fashioned icehouse, reportedly with the largest volume of any ice-chamber in Scotland.

STAGS ON KNOYDART PENINSULA

Above Stuck as it is between Heaven (the Lochs of Nevis) and Hell (Loch Hourn), it follows that Knoydart Peninsula would be Purgatory. At the moment it is certainly in a state of limbo, stuck between conservation or development as an area for tourists. Thanks to de-population in the nineteenth century, Knoydart Peninsula is a deserted lump of wilderness, but certain breeds of wildlife, such as the deer pictured here, thrive. The Highland red deer are free-ranging wild animals and most of them are descended from introduced European stock. The wild deer are a valuable asset to the Highland estate, as many people are prepared to pay large sums of money to hunt them.

STAGS

Right Hunting has become a political issue in Scotland, all too reminiscent of the Clearings. In many ways Scotland takes the preservation of its abundant wildlife very seriously. Stags and deer still wander freely in some parts of Scotland, but there are also specialized deer centres, such as the one in Cupar, set up to protect and rear the animals. Almost all visitors to the Scottish moors will see red deer, in season between 1 July and 20 October, or the roe deer with a more open season. In autumn, the stags become fiercely territorial and the air is full of their eerie cries. During the winter, however, deer favour the shelter of their ancestors and migrate to the wooded glens of the lower ground.

HEATHER AND PEAT

With uses ranging from thatching, rope weaving, tattie baskets, doormats, medicinal and culinary applications

and even wool dyeing, Scotland's most famous plant dominates much of the moorland area. The appearance of

heather changes according to season. In August, the plants blossom into the purple for which it is so well known,

but come the spring, the moors are littered with small burnt patches – the traditional way of maintaining the

moor. Peat is still used for fuel in some areas, but as it takes a year to form 5mm (quarter inch), the bogs of

decomposed vegetation are starting to run out. The crisscross pattern in this photograph is formed by the way

it is cut – 1-metre (3-ft) deep rectangular blocks are cut by hand using a *tairsgeir*, the Gaelic word for peat-iron.

TREES

For most people, the Highlands are synonymous with Scotland, a wilderness that is in turn both barren and plentiful. In fact, a large proportion of the Highland is covered by pine trees, which colonized land left bare after the end of the last Ice Age. However, the forestry is not simply a haphazard collection of naturally growing trees. Half of Britain's forestry is in Scotland, and forests like the one in the picture are very much man-made, hence the neat rows. They are grown for their timber, which is highly valued. This is not to say that trees are not highly regarded in Scotland – far from it. In 1992, the Scottish Natural Heritage was set up to cultivate a better understanding of the nature inherent in Scotland, in order to conserve the natural resources.

TREE PATTERNS

In 1998, a plan was put into place by Edinburgh MPs to encourage tree planting in Scotland called 'Trees of Time and Place'. Scots were encouraged to plant a tree to celebrate the new millennium, in order to make their nation a greener place in which to live. Maintaining the environment is an issue that is foremost in many people's minds. In this photograph, lush woods contrast starkly with an area of burnt heather, the traditional way of ensuring that each year the plant bears fresh new sprouts .

LOCH FLEET AND SAND DUNES

Left These two photographs may have different elements as their subject, but there is something of a similarity in the rippling way they undulate. If nature is your thing, you couldn't go wrong by visiting Loch Fleet. The area is so abundant in rich varieties of wildlife that most of it is a Scottish Wildlife Trust Reserve. It is home to Britain's densest concentration of St Olaf's candlestick, or one-flowered wintergreen, and the birdlife is also uncommonly diverse, attracting wigeon, goldeneye and shelduck in winter, and common and velvet divers in spring.

BANKS OF LOCHS EIL

Right Running by the banks of Loch Eil is Telford's Road, the namesake of the romantic *Road to the Isles* song, the chorus of which goes as follows:

'Sure, by Tummel and Loch Rannoch and Lochaber I will go.
By heather tracks wi' heaven in their wiles;
If it's thinkin' in your inner heart braggart's in my step,
You've never smelt the tangle O' the Isles.'

Lunan Bay

Packed with bizarre and unusual cave features, Lunan Bay is one of the only unspoilt natural bays in the British Isles and enjoys a good reputation for safe swimming. Situated to the south of Montrose, the sand of this east-facing horseshoe bay sweeps across two miles and is divided in the middle by Lunan Water. Lunan Bay is also the place where the spectre of Montrose, said to haunt the air museum, was killed. The ghost dates back to 1913, when Lieutenant Desmond Arthur's aircraft broke up over the bay and he was killed outright. Buried in Sleepyhillock cemetery, he is said to be responsible for spooky footsteps and rattling of doors dressed in uniform after being blamed for the crash, even though an inquest cleared his name.

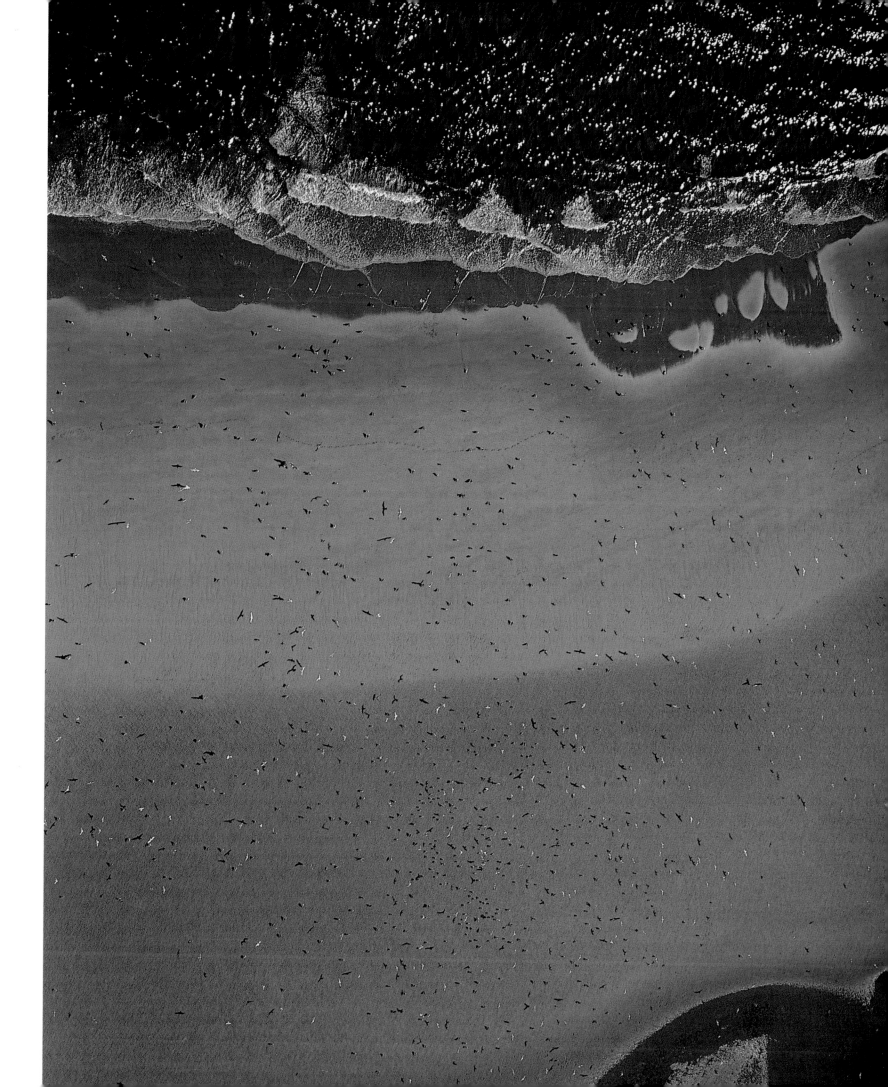

COASTLINES

A quick glance at any map of Scotland reveals a good indication that the shore here is far from smooth and these three photographs show differing views. Jagged cliffs give way to sheer drops and rocks splinter roughly into the water. Although the sea looks calm in these photos, you can imagine that it is not always so and the power of the water is, of course, responsible for shaping the land into the patterns seen here. Photographs of any three points of the coast would throw up similarities and differences, but the three here are Brough Head, Ord Point and Ness Head.

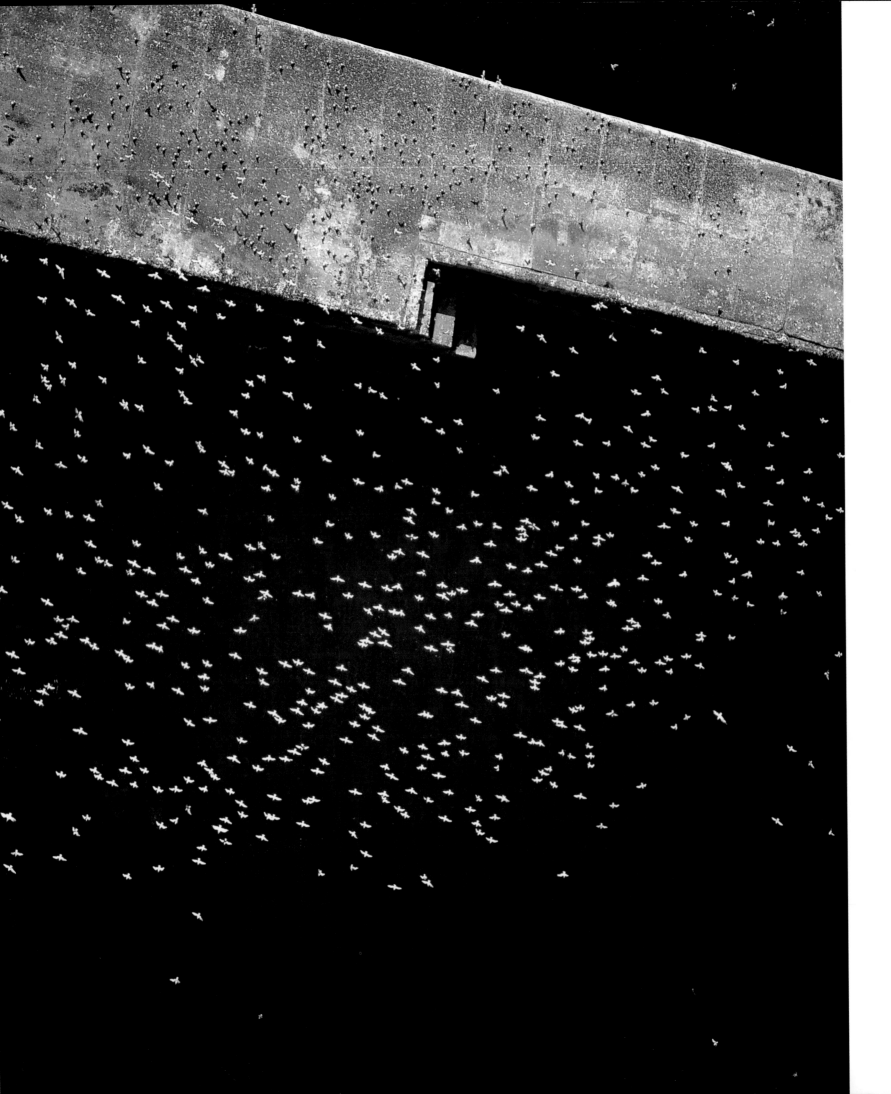

BIRDS OVER ABERDEEN DOCKS PIER

Left Scotland is a bird-watcher's paradise. There are an astonishing 80 bird reserves in total, mostly under the jurisdiction of the Royal Society for the Protection of Birds and the Nature Conservancy Council. The most spectacular bird colonies are found on the off-shore islands. For example, the Island of Rum, ironically often said to look like to a basket of eggs from a distance, is home to a large number of Manx shearwaters, which nest in the soft soils of the mountainside. Mainland birds include ospreys and golden eagles, who live in eyries raised up to 615m (2000ft) in the Highlands.

CANOES ON LOCH EIL

Above Here is a photograph of a group of canoeists who, it would appear by their haphazard positioning, have no idea of where they are heading.

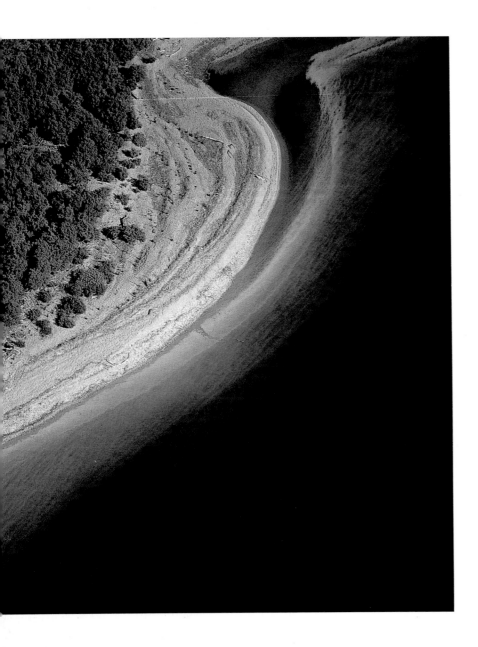

LOCH OICH

Above Loch Oich will always be overshadowed by its more famous counterpart Loch Ness, which it flows into. Nonetheless, Loch Oich is not only stunning but also has its own tale to tell. Near the southern tip of the loch is the Well of the Heads. The story goes that this well was built to commemorate the decapitation by the family bard of seven brothers who had murdered the two sons of a seventeenth-century chief of Clan Keppoch of the MacDonnell Clan. The heads were washed in the well before being presented to the chief of the MacDonnells at Glengarry.

LOCH FLEET

Right Situated by a pine wood, Loch Fleet is rich with Scottish wildlife. It is the place to go for birdwatching, as it is one of the country's most important bird reserves. Among those you could expect to see are peregrine, merlin, buzzard, wigeon, golden eagle, eider, oystercatcher, knot, red-breasted merganser, shelduck and curlew. The list is pretty much endless.

HARVEST FESTIVAL

Taken in late August, the weather conditions on the day this photograph was taken were necessarily clear and sunny. Anything else and the pilot wouldn't have taken off with a photographer in tow as the ground wouldn't be sufficiently visible beneath the helicopter. However, the weather in Scotland is well known for its unpredictabilty, and a single place can run the gauntlet from sun to rain in a matter of hours. Fortunately for the farmer at harvest time, the north of the country has an average of 18 to 20 hours of daylight in the height of summer, with the sun rising at 4am and setting at around 11.30pm, thus leaving the farmer plenty of time to harvest his fields in the light.

Harvested Fields

Covering the northern two-thirds of Scotland, people are often surprised by how remote the Highlands really are. Although not exactly untouched, the area offers unrivalled tranquility and the breadth of scenery is awe-inspiring, from glistening lochs to wooded glens and great mountains. Wildlife is abundant and man is rare, although the imprint of his past is everywhere. One example are the crumbling crofts, which hark back to the de-population of the eighteenth and nineteenth century, when land was cleared of people to make way for large-scale sheep farming. In the midst of this, fields of perfectly parallel lines stick out like a sore thumb and the eye is inevitably drawn to this tightly regimented pattern over some of the more spectacular natural features.

KINGS KNOT

Above Laid out beneath Stirling Castle is King's Knot, an octagonal stepped mound, which would have once formed part of a spectacular formal garden, complete with box trees and ornamental hedges. Dates vary as to when it was landscaped, but as it is set away from the castle it would have only been used in peaceful times, and so may have been laid out for a visit by Charles I in 1628. Today, just the earthworks survive and the mound is grassed over.

TELEGRAPH POLES

Right Just south of Edinburgh, this amazingly green field is subtly punctuated with the 'T'-shaped mark of technology. Telephone calls, faxes and internet connections each pass across the greatest of distances in less than a second, although in just a few years these small poles will probably be superceded by more obtrusive masts.

AROUND THE COAST

FROM SOUTHWEST TO SOUTHEAST

No doubt about it, with 130 inhabited islands and an irregularly shaped mainland, the one thing you are not short of in Scotland is vast stretches of coast. Diversity is key; the shore can be beguilingly beautiful, like the silver sands of Morar, or devastatingly dangerous – names of coves such as The Whaler and The Frenchmen are reminders of ships that ran aground here many years ago. The reputation of an unstable climate may prevent tourists being drawn to the beaches in their droves, but this does not mean they are lacking in beauty.

Inevitably, the water has played a strong role in the history, culture and industry of the country. Even the Gaelic words for whisky (*uisge beatha*) mean water of life. Scotland has long been established as the home of extremely fine salmon and Arbroath is famous for its 'smokies' (haddock flavoured and browned with smoke from an oak fire), but the fishing industry's heyday was unarguably the prosperous herring boom of the 1800s. Ports such as Dunbeath were set up by local lairds purely to take advantage of the excess of trade, and the employment it offered was vast. At its peak, Wick had more than 1000 herring boats working out of its complex of harbours and employed around 8000 people. It may have been prosperous, but it was also pure hard work. Boats would leave between 5 and 7pm and not return until around 3am. Once landed, the women would gut and pack the salted fish into barrels. The nets would be spread out to dry and the fishermen would have a few hours to get their heads down, before starting all over again.

When the local fishermen found they couldn't compete with larger boats and more advanced equipment, trade slumped. Today, most fishing ports are still in use although they are nowhere near as busy as they once were. The water still offers fishing in stunning locations, however, and is as popular as ever with recreational sailors, divers and windsurfers.

LARGS

Situated on the Firth of Clyde, Largs (*left*) is a family holiday resort with an emphasis on watersports – the Scottish National Watersports Centre is based here. Largs was the location for an 'accidental' battle, which took place in 1263 and is commemorated by a Pencil Monument about one mile south along the shoreline. It was accidental because the Vikings didn't mean to attack; their longships were simply blown ashore by stormy gales and the Scots ran through the surf to attack them. Let's hope that the little fishing boat in the picture above doesn't meet a similar fate.

BRODICK, ISLE OF ARRAN

Top right Brodick is the capital town on the oblong Isle of Arran, the most southerly of the Isles and therefore the most accessible. Today, with a reputation for healthy outdoor pursuits, it is a popular tourist resort although its elitist owners, the Dukes of Hamilton, tried to stave off this inevitability for as long as possible.

SALTCOATS

Bottom right Saltcoats town is on the west coast of lowland Scotland overlooking the Isle of Arran. Its name is taken from a past history of salt panning. Ferries from here run on their 55-minute journey to Brodick Bay on the east coast of Arran.

WEMYSS BAY

Opposite The Victorian train station that stands here harks back to a time when Glaswegians would have packed Wemyss Bay every summer on their holidays. Today, the ferry is the main mode of transport and it runs every hour to Rothersay, the only town on the Isle of Bute.

GLASGOW

There is a saying in Scotland that Edinburgh is the capital but Glasgow has the capital, a reference to the late nineteenth century when Glasgow was known as the 'Second City of the Empire'. Today it is extraordinarily well loved, with often-cited qualities including its cosmopolitan feel, the friendliness of the people and a large capacity for varying architectural styles. For example, the Art School was designed by one of Scotland's most celebrated architects, Charles Rennie Mackintosh, and the neo-Gothic building in the foreground of the main picture – Glasgow University – was designed by Sir George Gilbert Scott. The fortunes of Glasgow have been up and down over the years, since in was founded by St Mungo in 534 AD. However, it is gratifying to see that despite the toll of industry there is still enough nature to live up to its original name: Glas – ghu or 'dear green place'.

ISLE OF BUTE

Above Bute, severed from the Cowal peninsula by a meagre sliver of water, was its own county until 1975 when it was thrown in with Argyll. The freshwater Loch Fad basically slices the isle in two, resulting in the northern half of the isle being hilly and uninhabited, while the southern half is made up of lowland style farmland.

TARBERT

Right On the other hand, the peninsula of Kintyre (can anyone hear that name without thinking of the Paul McCartney song?) would be an island, if it wasn't for a mile-long isthmus between West and East Loch Tarbert. Backed by densely tree-covered hills, the village of Tarbert sits at the head of the East Loch and has a long tradition of fishing.

OBAN

Above Oban lies at the heart of the coastal region known as Lorn, after the Irish Celt Loarn who settled here *c.* 500 AD. As the largest port in northwest Scotland and the departure point for ferries to the Hebrides, the bay is always thronging with vessels.

THE MORAR PENINSULA

Left and right As one of the most beautiful stretches of coastline, the stunning silver sands of Morar comprise the most fantastic mesh of colour; a kaleidoscope of turquoise sea and orange seaweed draped over the rocks. The asymmetric jutting peninsula of Morar lies just south of Mallaig, and its loch, Britain's deepest body of fresh water, cuts straight across it. Legend has it that this is home to Nessie's less well known, but more foreboding counterpart, Morag. People do not try too hard to seek her out as it is said that her appearance signifies the death of a Clanranald Macdonald.

MALLAIG, SOUND OF SLEAT

Above As the most important herring and shellfish port in Britain and the west coast's principal fishing port, you would expect Mallaig to be a lively village, and it is. Mallaig is reached by the 'Road to the Isles', a road richly associated with Charles Edward Stuart. It may be the end of the road to the Isles, but it also a seaway to reach them as it the location for the car-ferry to Armadale on Skye.

DOUNE

Right Doune, on the irregularly shaped Knoydart Peninsula, is known as the last wilderness of Great Britain. Two hundred years ago, the population of Knoydart was around 1000 people. Today, just 70 inhabitants populate the 55,000 acres of space. The only way to get to there is by boat or undertaking a 20-mile hike as there is no road; not only does it feel miles from anywhere, it really is.

ISLE OF SKYE

Derived from the Norse word for cloud (*skuy*), Skye has now earned itself the Gaelic nickname *Eilean a Cheo*, or Island of Mist, due to the predictable unpredictability of its weather. Luckily, the breath-taking views from the island, coupled with the great hiking provided by the Cuillins and the bizarre rock formations of the Trotternish peninsula, more than compensate and so Skye has been a popular tourist destination since Victorian times. It is well known for being the hiding place of Bonnie Prince Charlie after his escape from Culloden, and today Skye is chock-full of places where he allegedly sat, hid or rested.

'Speed bonnie boat, like a bird on the wing,
"Onward" the sailors cry;
Carry the lad that's born to be king
Over the sea to Skye'

from *The Skye Boat Song* by HE BOULTON

THURSO

Above Another place that has gained its name from a Norse word is Thurso, meaning 'River of the God Thor'. During Viking times, it was used as a gateway to the mainland and was the principal trading port for Scandinavia. Although Thurso probably hit its heyday in the eleventh century, when it was an important Viking stronghold, it continued to prosper as a fishing port until the Second World War. Today, however, most of the town's employment comes from the atomic reactor along the coast at Dounreay.

DUNNET BAY

Right It's a common misconception that John O'Groats is the northernmost point of Scotland. The truth is that this accolade should be awarded to Dunnet Bay, a windy, lonely stretch of shoreline. It can't always have been so desolate; the area is dense with archaeological sites, and its history can be traced back 11,000 years to the Ice Age.

JOHN O' GROATS

Above The village of John O' Groats owes its name to a story first recorded in 1793. It tells of Dutchman Jan de Groot who settled there. He obtained the ferry contract for the crossing to Orkney in 1496 and built an eight-sided house for his eight quarrelling sons so that each could enter through his own door.

STACKS OF DUNCANSBY HEAD

Right Two miles east of John O'Groats is Duncansby Head. The sharp spikes of rock that serrate the sea are known as the Stacks and the thin, sheer-sided islets are locally called geos.

THE HIGHLANDS

A well-known symptom of aerial photography is that
height can appear to flatten even the most rocky of
terrains. However, flying north up the eastern coast of
Caithness, the ground really does dramatically level out
and the landscape, as shown in these three photographs,
undergoes a complete transformation. Gone are the
heather-blanketed moors, to be replaced with acre upon
acre of green horizontal plains. The vast fields, sliced
with chunky stone walls, are broken up only by the
occasional crumbling croft and the population becomes
noticeably increasingly sparse.

Coastline at Bruan

Above left The eastern coastline of the Highlands doesn't attract tourists to the same extent of the west coast, but the surrounding countryside has some extraordinary ancient remains. Just two miles north of this coastline is the 'Hill o' Many Stanes'. In keeping with the Scots tradition of calling a spade a spade, this is made up of 200 boulders, which form 22 parallel lines running north to south. Archaeological research has shown that there were originally 600 stones here, but like so many relics from the past no one knows what they where used for.

Lybster

Above right Lybster is still a relatively busy fishing port, but when it was built at the zenith of the nineteenth-century herring boom it had more than 200 working boats. The village may be surrounded by rather bleak moorland, but this is a countryside crammed full of ancient monuments. Just beyond Lybster are the Grey Cairns of Camster, two enormous prehistoric burial chambers thought to have been constructed 4500 years ago.

CLIFFS AT DUNBEATH

Left Between Latheron and Borgue lies the little village of Dunbeath, the birthplace of Neil Gunn (1891-1973). One of Scotland's foremost writers, his best known book is probably The Silver Darlings, and Gunn's writing reflects his own experiences growing up in the northeast during the great days of the herring industry boom. These days it is hard to reconcile the coast as he knew it with the sleepy harbour of today. This photograph was taken just south of Dunbeath, where the gigantic cliffs appear to be melting into the sea.

COASTLINE NEAR BERRIEDALE

Right Sculpted by the untameable Atlantic Ocean, the Caithness coastline is a craggy mixture of high sheer cliffs and more sheltered sandy beaches and secluded harbours. The ravages of the Clearances inland are still clearly obvious today in the desolate, treeless landscape. The main road for anyone driving through this part of the country climbs sharply up the Ord of Caithness. Before it was modernized into the all-new-and-improved version, this was not a journey for the faint-hearted, as the seaward precipices were apparently nerve-wracking.

HELMSDALE

One of the many villages to have been developed to take advantage of the herring boom of the last century, Helmsdale sits at the mouth of one of the north's great salmon rivers and is surrounded by steep hills and croftland. It was devised as a fishing/farming community by the Duke of Sutherland who divided the crofters into two groups to take care of the sea and land. Just like nearby Lybster (see page 69), fishing still provides a decent trade but the boom-days have long gone. The rocky shoreline is a well-known finding place for fossils and gemstones, but if it's gold you're after, try Baile an Or, whose name is Gaelic for 'Goldfield'. Just eight miles up the river, this precious metal was discovered in 1869, resulting in quite a gold rush.

FORTROSE, MORAY FIRTH

Left In the seventeenth century, the seemingly peaceful village of Fortrose was home to the Brahan Seer, whose prophecies foretold of the Clearances and the Second World War. His talent was also his demise, as is so often the way, and began when Lady Seaford asked him to use his gift to track down her wayward husband. Brahan Seer 'saw' her husband in the arms of another woman, and in a rage Lady Seaford ordered Seer's execution by being boiled in a barrel of tar.

INVERNESS

Right The location of this town has had an impact on everything about it: its name, its trade and its importance. The word Inverness derives from Inbhir, meaning the 'mouth' of the River Ness. The original settlement was established around 5000 years ago, when the steep hills and difficult to navigate water forced people to pass through a bottleneck, and it soon became an important trade route. As always, trade brought with it the two-edged sword of prosperity and constant threat of attack, especially from marauding Highlanders. After all, he who controlled the ford, controlled the gateway to the Northern Highlands.

Aberdeen

By the thirteenth century, Aberdeen had become a thriving mercantile centre and a quietly important port, but it wasn't until the late 1800s that the city experienced its first boom. By building the Aberdeen Clippers, the shipyards totally revolutionized sea transport and when a group of local businessmen got hold of a steam tugboat, trawl fishing really took off and plenty of fisher families moved in. Two hundred years later, Aberdeen experienced another huge boom when oil was discovered, although this looked set to come to an end with the double whammy of an oil price slump and the Piper Alpha disaster. Today, the oil trade is more stable, and, love it or hate it, this granite city is going from strength to strength.

STONEHAVEN

Left With its eighteenth- and nineteenth-century town centre, the sandy beaches of Stonehaven are never short of a visitor of two. The gently curving bays are divided in two by the harbour, with the fishing port on the south side, and it offers good sailing as well as a base for sea angling. With fingers in the pies of agriculture, manufacture and tourists, the fishing today involves only small craft and for recreational rather than trade. Nevertheless, both the harbour and the surrounding area contain the roots of a seafaring heritage crammed with folklore and ancient tradition, which hark back to Stonehaven's golden years.

MONTROSE

Above Thanks to the medieval church, which was previously built on the site of the present Old Church, the Angus town of Montrose has a history that traces back to the thirteenth century. It has seen both peaceful and turbulent times, as it played a prominent part in the reformation and was the scene for the bloodiest naval battle of the war in 1746.

MONIFIETH, DUNDEE

Left On the outskirts on Dundee, Monifieth offers a golf course and wide sands of beach with wonderful views across the Tay Estuary. However, the chief attraction is the fact that the area is dotted with Souterrains. These earth houses date to the Iron Age, and are thought to have been used as homes, farm buildings, ritual sites and hiding places. The remains show that the structures where quite sophisticated with stone drains and even the remnants of a water tank where the inhabitant probably kept shellfish.

DUNDEE CITY CENTRE

Right top With a population of around 150,000 and two universities, 10 per cent of the city of Dundee's inhabitants are students and so Dundee has gained a reputation for being a historic city that is young at heart. Gazing south over the Tay Estuary, the city of Dundee has long been known for its economic reliance on jute (a type of linen). As a global manufacturing centre, the Dundee fabric travelled as far afield as the American West where it provided the cover for the wagon trains that carried pioneers.

DOCKS AT DUNDEE

Right Dundee was established as a small fishing and boat building community in the Middle Ages, but prospered from jute and jam until the town was devastated by General Monks' New Model Army in 1651. The city fell back on local skills and grew to become a major ship building port, with famous examples, such as *HM Frigate* Unicorn, still berthed in the docks.

NEWPORT-ON-TAY

Left With a population of around 3000, Newport-on-Tay is really a small town but the locals still like to think of it as a village. Unfortunately, Newport's place in history is marked in John Wesley's diary as the village where no one would offer him food or lodging on his long journey south.

ST ANDREWS TOWN AND GOLF COURSE

Above and right Scotland is well known as the home of the game of golf. When 22 noblemen decided to move their golf games to St Andrews in 1754 it was the saving grace of the town and the very first golf course ever created is thought to be the Old Course.

EDINBURGH CITY CENTRE

'Edinburgh is what Paris ought to be'

ROBERT LOUIS STEVENSON (1850-1894)

Born and bred in Edinburgh, Stevenson loved his hometown and his soundbites on the subject are eminently quotable and, indeed, endlessly quoted. Among them, he expressed surprise that the city was not 'a dropscene in a theatre, but a city in the world of everyday reality'. In the photograph opposite the architectural divide of the city is clearly seen where Princes Street runs between the two, just north of Waverley Station. To the south is the labyrinth of narrow streets and seamy alleys of the Old Town, and north is the elegant neo-classical New Town, built in the eighteenth century because the old town was overcrowded and malodorous. No prizes for guessing which side was the inspiration for Stevenson's infamous Dr Jeckyll and Mr Hyde. The picture to the left shows North Bridge running north from a closer detail of Old Town and bisecting Waverley Station.

THE INTERIOR

PLACES ARE OFTEN inextricably linked with myths, legends and stories, and the central parts of Scotland are no different. From Loch Ness to Bonnie Prince Charlie, the interior of Scotland is bursting with history and the most serene of places can have a bloody tale to tell. Who would guess that the beautiful mountain valley of Glen Coe was once the site of a notorious massacre? In 1692, around 45 people were slain and many others died of exposure when the Macdonalds were victims of a long-standing government desire to suppress the clans. Even the Borders, once the bloodstained location for interminable warfare between the English and the Scots, is now a fertile, peaceful region.

Inland, the countryside is every bit as diverse as the coastline would suggest; a riot of sparkling lochs, beautiful oak woodlands, breathtaking hills and mountains as well as the most desolate of terrains. As you would expect, the ravages of the Clearances are brutally clear and it is extraordinary how there is nothing shocking about looking at a deserted hill until you realize that a full community once thrived here.

What is it that makes Scotland so magnificent? Perhaps it is simply that it is a land of contrast. Scotland is often admired for its mountains; there are 279 distinct peaks over 923m (3000ft) (known as Munros after the mountaineer who first classified them), and the number includes the infamous Ben Nevis, the highest peak in Britain at 1355m (4406ft). Granted, the higher slopes of the mountains are often refuges for rare Arctic and Alpine plants, but, even so, they are nothing special when compared to others. What makes the mountains so awe-inspiring is that they are in a country where the land is also deeply gorged with lochs, where some areas are peppered with castles and towns while others are nothing more than wide open spaces, and where majestic hills coincide with velvet-green valleys.

LANDSCAPE SOUTH OF KEELS AND LOCH FLEET

Broadly speaking, Scotland consists of three main geographical regions: the Highlands, the Central Lowlands and the Southern Uplands. The term 'Lowlands' is something of a misnomer, however, as it comprises rolling hill ranges as well as the more expected undulating farmland. The Southern Uplands mirror the Lowlands to an extent; although they are usually described as 'gentler', they still include seven major hill ranges. As part of the Borders (and therefore the Uplands), this landscape shot close to Keels (*left*) certainly appears both gentle and serene. Loch Fleet too (*above*), while known for the rich diversity of its wildlife, looks perfectly still and at peace.

INNERLEITHEN

The following extract was printed in the *Imperial Gazetteer of Scotland*, edited by John Marius Wilson and published by A. Fullarton & Co. in 1868:

'The hills are cloven asunder from north to south by several deep glens, each bringing down the tribute of a crystal stream to the Tweed ... The course of the Tweed majestically sweeps along the southern boundary [and] is exquisitely beautiful ... [Though] a stranger might suppose the interior to be a hilly wilderness of rocks and desolation, yet the southern exposure of the general surface occasions the growth of much excellent sheep-pasturage.' Today the village of Innerleithen is more developed, but its surroundings haven't changed a bit.

River Tay

The River Tay, here pictured near Perth, is one of the premier salmon rivers of Europe. These days, salmon as large as 13.3kg (30lb) are caught on Scotland's rivers each year, but it is the Tay that boasts the British record – a fish of 28.5kg (64lb) caught by a Miss Ballantyne in 1922. In recent years, there have been worries that the fish for which Scotland is so famous may be in need of preservation, so the Tay has dramatically reduced fishing pressure by removing most of the system nets that were in place. The salmon's only real danger now is from rod anglers, of whom many obey various rules as a precaution, such as no fishing on Sunday and a voluntary catch and release scheme.

Perth

Built up around the banks of the Tay, Scotland's longest river, Perth was the gateway to the Highlands for many centuries. Its location ensured its success as a trading port and claret from Bordeaux was imported while salmon and wool were exported, and for a time it was the capital of Scotland. In the opening pages of his novel, *The Fair Maid of Perth*, Sir Walter Scott writes of approaching the town from the south: '… the town of Perth with its two large measures or inches, its steeples and towers; the hills of Moncreiff and Kinnoul faintly rising into picturesque rocks, partly clothed with woods; the rich margin of the river studded with elegant mansions; and the huge Grampian Mountains, the northern screen of this exquisite landscape.'

KELSO, RIVER TWEED

Left To remain in the mind-set of Sir Walter Scott for just a minute longer, he attributed Kelso with being the most beautiful, if not the most romantic, town in Scotland. This cobbled town in the heart of the Scottish Borders has a population of just 6000 people, but boasts a thriving community nonetheless. While a casual visitor would find it easy to forget less peaceful times, the surrounding countryside cannot and is peppered with castles, fortified towers, keeps and the remains of the Border abbeys, all of which are testament to a more turbulent history.

JEDBURGH

Right Nestled in the valley of the Jed Water on the edge of the wild Cheviot Hills, Jedburgh is best known for its impressive, if roofless, abbey. The abbey dates back to the twelfth century and dominates the town. In the foreground of this photograph is the Castle Jail. A favourite residence for royalty during the twelfth century, the castle was pulled down by the townsfolk to prevent it falling into English hands. Rebuilt as a Howard Reform Prison in 1823, the jail was considered to be one of the most modern jails of its time and the building as it stands today is the only existing example of its kind in Scotland.

LOCH MORAR AND LOCH LOMOND

If Loch Morar is famous for its monster (see page 59 and *left*), then Loch Lomond (*above*) must be famous for

the following extract from the well-known Jacobite folksong:

'By you bonny banks and you bonny braes,
Where the sun shines bright on Loch Lomond,
Where me and my true love were ever wont to gae,
On the bonny, bonny banks of Loch Lomond.

'O you'll take the high road and I'll take the low road
And I'll be in Scotland afore ye,
But me and my true love will never meet again
On the bonny, bonny banks of Loch Lomond.

''Twas there that we parted in yon shady glen,
On the steep, steep side of Loch Lomond,
Where deep in purple hue the Highland hills we view,
And the moon coming out in the gloaming.'

LOCH FLEET

The reason there are so many pictures of this loch in this book is simply because it is the photographer's favourite place in Scotland. It is not hard to see why, and the addition of so much truly wild, unusual and varied nature doesn't harm matters at all. Lochs in Scotland have similar features to Scandinavian fjords, and it is thought that they originated the same way. Because of their depth, it is assumed that they are of glacial origin. The enormous glaciers that formed in these valleys were so heavy they eroded the bottom of the valley way below sea level before they floated in the ocean water. Once the glaciers melted, the sea water invaded the valleys.

LOCH NESS

Above Loch Ness is, of course, synonymous with the beloved Nessie, the Loch Ness Monster. From St Columba to the twentieth century, the possibility of an unidentified creature living in the loch has ensured plenty of casual 'sightings', more scientific research and a lot of media speculation. The fact that the loch is one of the largest in Scotland with a volume of 7500 million cubic metres, and a bottom, which for 15 miles lies 160m (520ft) below sea level, means that the loch is far from easy to explore and could be one of the reasons imaginations have been so inflamed.

LOCH DUICH

Right There have been no sightings of monsters in Loch Duich, but its deep and peaceful waters are nevertheless a favourite diving spot for locals and visitors alike. Small clusters of boulders hide a multitude of sea life including scorpion fish, butterfish, queen scallops, lightbulb sea squirts, peacock worms, cuttlefish and dragonets.

RAILWAY VIADUCT AT GLENFINNAN

Glenfinnan will strike a chord with most Scots, thanks to the story of Bonnie Prince Charlie's fight for the British throne. Having raised his standard to signal the start of the Jacobite uprising, his wait was finally over when on 19 August 1745 Cameron of Loch Sheil and his troops came marching down the valley. The long reaches of Loch Sheil are veiled by rolling green mountains and the rallying of some 1000 Highlanders must have been an incredible sight. Furthermore, Glenfinnan has received recognition for its imposing 21-arched viaduct, which carries trains across a 300-m (1000-ft) span. More than 30m (100ft) above the ground, the viaduct was built in 1901 and was one of the first large constructions to be made out of concrete.

Loch Alsh

Left The rolling mountains that surround Loch Alsh are formed by some of the world's oldest rocks, dating back more than 2600 million years, and the loch itself was gouged out around 1 million years ago by glaciers in the Ice Age. In this picture, the water looks beautifully serene, disturbed by only the merest of ripples.

Salmon Nets on Loch Duich

Above Ranking among the cleanest coasts in Europe, fishing has always been a favourite pastime in Scotland and has been enjoyed recreationally as well as industrially. Despite its abundance of good fishing spots, there are not the crowds of anglers you would expect. There are salmon in almost all of Scotland's rivers and in many of the lochs, but pollution has taken its toll on Scotland's best loved fish, and conservation projects have been put into place to ensure their continued abundance.

SEALS ON ISLAND IN LOCH NEVIS

Left You would imagine that Loch Nevis and Ben Nevis would be close to each other. Not so, there are 50 miles between them. Funnily enough, even the name 'Nevis' does not necessarily mean the same thing. Loch Nevis is taken to mean 'the Loch of Heaven', whereas most believe that Ben Nevis means 'venomous' or 'malicious', due to the fury of the Atlantic storms it can sometimes evoke.

INVERIE

Right Until the notorious Clearances (see page 9), the wild, inhospitable Knoydart peninsula was home to around a thousand people who made a living by crofting and fishing. The population saw a dramatic reduction when evictions started in 1853, as the new landowners ran the land as a playground for hunting and shooting. This sparked off a land raid in the 1940s by the 'Seven men of Knoydart' who 'staked their claims and were digging their drains/On Brocket's private land', as the Hamish Henderson ballad goes. Although their valiant attempt to reclaim their land failed, the crofters of Knoydart finally regained ownership of their land in a community buy-out in 1998. Today, of the 70 inhabitants who live there, most live in the tiny settlement of Inverie.

Moidart and Lismore Island in Loch Linnhe

In contrast to the barrenness of the photograph of Moidart (*above*), the fertility of the Island of Lismore (*right*) gave birth to its name (*leis mor* is Gaelic for 'the big garden'). Legend has it that St Columba was in a race with St Moluag to land on the island and found a monastery. Such was St Moluag's religious determination that he cut off his finger and threw it onto the shore. This desperate measure gave him possession of the island and today the cathedral of St Moluag occupies the site of the church that he founded.

LOCH SUNART

Left In the 1800s, Loch Sunart was the location of a floating church. During the 'Disruption', the free church broke away from the Church of Scotland. With no ground to set up a new worship place – the local laird stoutly refused to house them on his land – the rebel group bought an old ship on the Clyde, re-fitted it and towed it to Loch Sunart. Protected by the freedom of the seas, this little congregation rowed around their 'parish' for around 30 years.

THE ISLE OF MULL

Right Below the light mists of low clouds is the Hebridean Isle of Mull. It suffered as much as anywhere during the Clearances and, exacerbated by the potato famine of 1846, the population has declined from 10,600 in 1820 to around 2400 today. Few of these people are natives to the island, and the English and Scottish newcomers are sometimes referred to pejoratively as the 'white settlers'. Each summer the population swells with students studying geology, archaeologists examining prehistoric sights and the endless drip of tourism. Year round, the island is alive with nature; there are around 3000 red deer (more than there are people), and wild white goats, polecats, stoats, mink, ferrets and otters are all common sights.

HILL TOPS AT MORVERN AND GLEN MORE

The tips of hill tops peaking through the swirling clouds give a dreamscape quality
to these pictures. The Morvern peninsula is a world away from the madding crowds
generally to be found at Glencoe or Ben Nevis, and as one of the most beautiful but
least-known areas of the west coast is a hillwalker's paradise.

SNOW-CAPPED MOUNTAINS, GLEN MORISTON

Above If it is serious peaks you are after, look no further than Glen Moriston, close to Loch Cluanie. The snow-capped mountains are rugged, awesome and show little sign of human habitation.

GARGUNNOCK HILLS

Right Even though the distinctive shapes of the Gargunnocks are due to ancient lava flows, this is an area of velvet-green rolling hills and wonderfully fertile farmland. Southwest of Stirling, people here are few and far between although there are a few picturesque villages nestling in the hills.

GETTING AROUND

Scotland's natural layout does not lend itself to being an easy place to travel around. Although the remoter areas of the Highlands can still be difficult to negotiate, increased tourism has inevitably led to constantly improved and updated routes and public transport. Drivers are appeased by the fabulous vistas from the coastal roads, and if you get bored of travelling overland there are a multitude of ferries on hand to whisk you away to one of the many surrounding islands.

Over the years, many Scots have played a role in building inventions involving transport. The first practical steamboat was built by William Synington on the River Clyde and was called the *Charlotte Dundas*. Henry Bell's *Comet* was the first commercial steamboat in Europe to carry passengers when she set sail on her maiden voyage from Glasgow to Greenock in August 1812. Robert Wilson invented the screw propeller in 1827 and Kirkpatrick Macmillan is credited with the invention of the first

pedal cycle in 1839. Unfortunately, not all the creations have been successes. On 28 December 1879, the central navigation spans of the Tay Bridge collapsed into the Firth of Tay at Dundee, taking with them a train, six carriages and 75 people. The bridge had only been open for 19 months and its collapse shocked both the Victorian engineering profession and general public. To date it is still the worst structural engineering failure in the British Isles.

This last chapter brings together photographs of a variety of man-made objects associated with travel, both by land and by sea. Aerial photography can transform our impressions of our surroundings, which is the essence of its impact. The photographer Edward Steichen wrote in 1918 that a print taken from the air 'badly represents nature from an angle we do not know.' To write this is to claim that the camera lies – but then again, you must make up your own mind after looking at these images.

NEPTUNE'S STAIRCASE AT BANAVIE, FORT WILLIAM

Left At the evocatively named Neptune's Staircase, the Caledonian Canal climbs an impressive 20m (64ft) in less than half a mile. The eight locks may not look steep from this angle, but at ground level they are quite punishing.

TOUR BOAT ON LOCH NESS

Above How many of the passengers enjoying this boat ride are secretly hoping to re-create the incident in 1933, when 30 guests from a nearby hotel witnessed an unexplainable sighting of a large creature playing in the loch?

FIRTH OF FORTH RAIL BRIDGE

After the tragic collapse of the Tay Bridge (see page 115) there was a need to regain the public's confidence and so the Firth of Forth Bridge was over-constructed and heavily so. Completed in 1890, the cantilever bridge boasted the longest span in the world, and even today it is the second longest of its kind. Designed and built by Benjamin Baker (1840-1907) the cost of the bridge was an extraordinary £2.5 million. It took seven years, 58,000 tons of steel, 18,122 cubic metres of granite, 8 million rivets and the loss of 57 lives before the bridge was complete. In the background of both of these photographs stands the Forth Road Bridge, a suspension bridge that was subsequently built in 1964.

KESSOCK BRIDGE, MORAY FIRTH

Left and top right The cable-stayed Kessock Bridge, which is 900m (3000ft) long, carries the A9 dual carriageway over the Beauly Firth to the north of Inverness. Before it opened, motorists travelling to Invergordon or the northeast had to queue for a small ferry, which could take a serious amount of time.

TAY BRIDGE, DUNDEE

Right For all the genius that Scotland has nurtured and inspired, there has to be a flipside and it comes in the package of the poet William McGonagall. It's not a great accolade, admittedly, but McGonagall is generally thought to be Scotland's worst poet. Before this sparks off any feelings of sympathy, read this extract from his cheerful little ditty about the Tay Bridge Disaster of 1879:

'So the train mov'd slowly along the Bridge of Tay,
Until it was about midway,
Then the central girders with a crash gave way,
And down went the train and passengers into the Tay!'

CAR FERRY AND TUG PULLING BOAT

Left and bottom left If aerial photography is all about perception, then it follows that different people will interpret images in different ways. From this bird's eye view, the cars driving on to the ferry at Wemyss Bay, ready to be taken across to the Isle of Bute, look no bigger than a child's toys. Below, the wake that the tug leaves behind as it pulls the second boat close to Aberdeen docks is like looking up at the streak of white that aeroplanes leave in the sky. Perhaps this is the power of aerial photography; our ceiling is now our pavement.

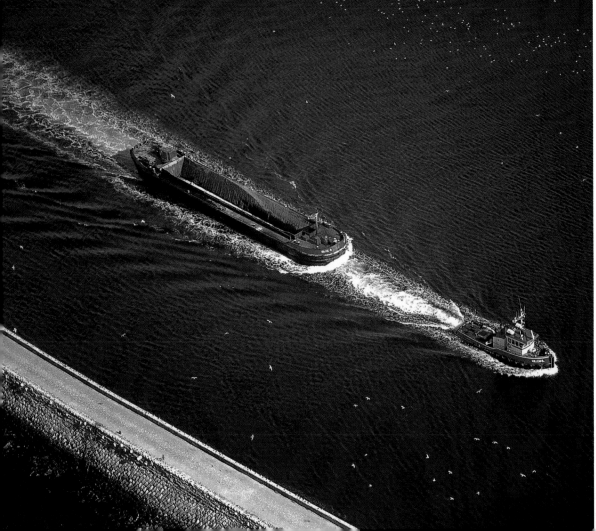

LIGHTHOUSE, HOLY ISLAND, JUST OFF ISLE OF ARRAN

Right Engineered by David and Thomas Stevenson, Holy Island Inner Lighthouse was built off the Isle of Arran in 1877. For many years, the goats had Holy Island to themselves but it has been owned by the Samye Ling Tibetan Center in Dumfries since 1992. Buddhist monks and nuns live in the lighthouse keeper's accommodation and the island is no longer open to the public.

OIL RIGS ON CROMARTY FIRTH

As a perfect natural harbour sheltered by the headlands of the Sutor rocks, Cromarty Firth has, arguably, the most diverse range of uses not only in Scotland but in all of Britain. It became an important naval base during the First World War; the majority of the giant North Sea oil rigs come here for maintenance; drilling rigs stay here when not under contract, and its excellent anchorage mean it is a premier location for everything from the QE2 (in 1994), to ferries, cargo ships and small pleasure crafts from the local yacht club. In contrast with the modern constructions of oil rigs at Nigg, the area has been awarded a host of National, European and International designations in recognition of its importance to birdlife and the local dolphin population.

THE ROADS TO THE ISLES

Above This photograph shows the A9 just north of Helmsdale, which hugs the coastline across the Moray, Cromarty and Dornock Firths until it reaches Latheron. Here it heads inland to Thurso. A major thoroughfare through the Highlands, the A9 has recently been upgraded as it helps to bring benefits such as tourism to a rural community. It is deemed sufficiently important to warrant the necessity of a Highland Host group, whose aims are to obtain informative sign postings for bypassed settlements and to ensure that non-commercial facilities such as picnic areas, toilets and telephones are provided along the way.

Right This slithering snake of a road is the A68 taken just across the border dividing England and Scotland, looking north. To the right of this road, and just out of sight, is Carter Bay. A popular place to stop and admire the view, it is also home to a resident bagpipe player.

PIPE FABRICATION FACILITY AT
SINCLAIR'S BAY

Left Transportation of offshore oil production to land-based storage has long been a difficult problem to solve. Using tankers is expensive and time-consuming so pipes have begun to be installed. The building pictured here is owned by Rockwell Ltd, who are currently building pipelines in up to four-and-a-half mile sections.

THE SOUND OF SLEAT

Above Looking across the Sound of Sleat from the mainland, you can see the outline of the Isle of Skye. The largest of the Hebridean islands, Skye is almost 50 miles long and between 7 and 25 miles wide. As the final picture in this aerial portrait of Scotland, it is fitting that the book should close on a such a particularly beautiful golden sunset.

INDEX